PHONE BOOK

NAME	

PHONE BOOK

NAME	PHONE NUMBER

THIS PASSWORD
BOOK BELONGS TO:

NAME: _____

PHONE: _____

EMAIL: _____

ISBN: 978-1-949781-27-4

PHONE BOOK

NAME	PHONE NUMBER

NAME:

WEBSITE:

EMAIL USED:

USERNAME:

PASSWORD:

PIN:

NOTES:

NAME:

WEBSITE:

EMAIL USED:

USERNAME:

PASSWORD:

PIN:

NOTES:

NAME:

WEBSITE:

EMAIL USED:

USERNAME:

PASSWORD:

PIN:

NOTES:

A

NAME:

WEBSITE:

EMAIL USED:

USERNAME:

PASSWORD:

PIN:

NOTES:

....

....

NAME:

WEBSITE:

EMAIL USED:

USERNAME:

PASSWORD:

PIN:

NOTES:

....

....

NAME:

WEBSITE:

EMAIL USED:

USERNAME:

PASSWORD:

PIN:

NOTES:

....

....

A

NAME:

WEBSITE:

EMAIL USED:

USERNAME:

PASSWORD:

PIN:

NOTES:

....

....

....

NAME:

WEBSITE:

EMAIL USED:

USERNAME:

PASSWORD:

PIN:

NOTES:

....

....

....

NAME:

WEBSITE:

EMAIL USED:

USERNAME:

PASSWORD:

PIN:

NOTES:

....

....

....

NAME: _____

WEBSITE: _____

EMAIL USED: _____

USERNAME: _____

PASSWORD: _____

PIN: _____

NOTES: _____

_____

_____

NAME: _____

WEBSITE: _____

EMAIL USED: _____

USERNAME: _____

PASSWORD: _____

PIN: _____

NOTES: _____

_____

_____

NAME: _____

WEBSITE: _____

EMAIL USED: _____

USERNAME: _____

PASSWORD: _____

PIN: _____

NOTES: _____

_____

_____

A

NAME:

WEBSITE:

EMAIL USED:

USERNAME:

PASSWORD:

PIN:

NOTES:

....

....

....

NAME:

WEBSITE:

EMAIL USED:

USERNAME:

PASSWORD:

PIN:

NOTES:

....

....

....

NAME:

WEBSITE:

EMAIL USED:

USERNAME:

PASSWORD:

PIN:

NOTES:

....

....

....

NAME: _____

WEBSITE: _____

EMAIL USED: _____

USERNAME: _____

PASSWORD: _____

PIN: _____

NOTES: _____

_____

_____

NAME: _____

WEBSITE: _____

EMAIL USED: _____

USERNAME: _____

PASSWORD: _____

PIN: _____

NOTES: _____

_____

_____

NAME: _____

WEBSITE: _____

EMAIL USED: _____

USERNAME: _____

PASSWORD: _____

PIN: _____

NOTES: _____

_____

_____

B

NAME:

WEBSITE:

EMAIL USED:

USERNAME:

PASSWORD:

PIN:

NOTES:

....

....

....

NAME:

WEBSITE:

EMAIL USED:

USERNAME:

PASSWORD:

PIN:

NOTES:

....

....

....

NAME:

WEBSITE:

EMAIL USED:

USERNAME:

PASSWORD:

PIN:

NOTES:

....

....

....

B

NAME:

WEBSITE:

EMAIL USED:

USERNAME:

PASSWORD:

PIN:

NOTES:

NAME:

WEBSITE:

EMAIL USED:

USERNAME:

PASSWORD:

PIN:

NOTES:

NAME:

WEBSITE:

EMAIL USED:

USERNAME:

PASSWORD:

PIN:

NOTES:

NAME:

WEBSITE:

EMAIL USED:

USERNAME:

PASSWORD:

PIN:

NOTES:

NAME:

WEBSITE:

EMAIL USED:

USERNAME:

PASSWORD:

PIN:

NOTES:

NAME:

WEBSITE:

EMAIL USED:

USERNAME:

PASSWORD:

PIN:

NOTES:

NAME:

WEBSITE:

EMAIL USED:

USERNAME:

PASSWORD:

PIN:

NOTES:

NAME:

WEBSITE:

EMAIL USED:

USERNAME:

PASSWORD:

PIN:

NOTES:

NAME:

WEBSITE:

EMAIL USED:

USERNAME:

PASSWORD:

PIN:

NOTES:

NAME: _____

WEBSITE: _____

EMAIL USED: _____

USERNAME: _____

PASSWORD: _____

PIN: _____

NOTES: ···

···

···

NAME: _____

WEBSITE: _____

EMAIL USED: _____

USERNAME: _____

PASSWORD: _____

PIN: _____

NOTES: ···

···

···

NAME: _____

WEBSITE: _____

EMAIL USED: _____

USERNAME: _____

PASSWORD: _____

PIN: _____

NOTES: ···

···

···

NAME:

WEBSITE:

EMAIL USED:

USERNAME:

PASSWORD:

PIN:

NOTES:

NAME:

WEBSITE:

EMAIL USED:

USERNAME:

PASSWORD:

PIN:

NOTES:

NAME:

WEBSITE:

EMAIL USED:

USERNAME:

PASSWORD:

PIN:

NOTES:

NAME:

WEBSITE:

EMAIL USED:

USERNAME:

PASSWORD:

PIN:

NOTES:

NAME:

WEBSITE:

EMAIL USED:

USERNAME:

PASSWORD:

PIN:

NOTES:

NAME:

WEBSITE:

EMAIL USED:

USERNAME:

PASSWORD:

PIN:

NOTES:

NAME:

WEBSITE:

EMAIL USED:

USERNAME:

PASSWORD:

PIN:

NOTES:

NAME:

WEBSITE:

EMAIL USED:

USERNAME:

PASSWORD:

PIN:

NOTES:

NAME:

WEBSITE:

EMAIL USED:

USERNAME:

PASSWORD:

PIN:

NOTES:

NAME:

WEBSITE:

EMAIL USED:

USERNAME:

PASSWORD:

PIN:

NOTES:

NAME:

WEBSITE:

EMAIL USED:

USERNAME:

PASSWORD:

PIN:

NOTES:

NAME:

WEBSITE:

EMAIL USED:

USERNAME:

PASSWORD:

PIN:

NOTES:

NAME:

WEBSITE:

EMAIL USED:

USERNAME:

PASSWORD:

PIN:

NOTES:

NAME:

WEBSITE:

EMAIL USED:

USERNAME:

PASSWORD:

PIN:

NOTES:

NAME:

WEBSITE:

EMAIL USED:

USERNAME:

PASSWORD:

PIN:

NOTES:

NAME:

WEBSITE:

EMAIL USED:

USERNAME:

PASSWORD:

PIN:

NOTES:

....

....

....

NAME:

WEBSITE:

EMAIL USED:

USERNAME:

PASSWORD:

PIN:

NOTES:

....

....

....

NAME:

WEBSITE:

EMAIL USED:

USERNAME:

PASSWORD:

PIN:

NOTES:

....

....

....

E

NAME:

WEBSITE:

EMAIL USED:

USERNAME:

PASSWORD:

PIN:

NOTES:

NAME:

WEBSITE:

EMAIL USED:

USERNAME:

PASSWORD:

PIN:

NOTES:

NAME:

WEBSITE:

EMAIL USED:

USERNAME:

PASSWORD:

PIN:

NOTES:

NAME:

WEBSITE:

EMAIL USED:

USERNAME:

PASSWORD:

PIN:

NOTES:

NAME:

WEBSITE:

EMAIL USED:

USERNAME:

PASSWORD:

PIN:

NOTES:

NAME:

WEBSITE:

EMAIL USED:

USERNAME:

PASSWORD:

PIN:

NOTES:

NAME:

WEBSITE:

EMAIL USED:

USERNAME:

PASSWORD:

PIN:

NOTES:

NAME:

WEBSITE:

EMAIL USED:

USERNAME:

PASSWORD:

PIN:

NOTES:

NAME:

WEBSITE:

EMAIL USED:

USERNAME:

PASSWORD:

PIN:

NOTES:

NAME:

WEBSITE:

EMAIL USED:

USERNAME:

PASSWORD:

PIN:

NOTES:

NAME:

WEBSITE:

EMAIL USED:

USERNAME:

PASSWORD:

PIN:

NOTES:

NAME:

WEBSITE:

EMAIL USED:

USERNAME:

PASSWORD:

PIN:

NOTES:

NAME:

WEBSITE:

EMAIL USED:

USERNAME:

PASSWORD:

PIN:

NOTES:

....

....

....

NAME:

WEBSITE:

EMAIL USED:

USERNAME:

PASSWORD:

PIN:

NOTES:

....

....

....

NAME:

WEBSITE:

EMAIL USED:

USERNAME:

PASSWORD:

PIN:

NOTES:

....

....

....

NAME:

WEBSITE:

EMAIL USED:

USERNAME:

PASSWORD:

PIN:

NOTES:

....

....

....

NAME:

WEBSITE:

EMAIL USED:

USERNAME:

PASSWORD:

PIN:

NOTES:

....

....

....

NAME:

WEBSITE:

EMAIL USED:

USERNAME:

PASSWORD:

PIN:

NOTES:

....

....

....

NAME:

WEBSITE:

EMAIL USED:

USERNAME:

PASSWORD:

PIN:

NOTES:

NAME:

WEBSITE:

EMAIL USED:

USERNAME:

PASSWORD:

PIN:

NOTES:

NAME:

WEBSITE:

EMAIL USED:

USERNAME:

PASSWORD:

PIN:

NOTES:

NAME:

WEBSITE:

EMAIL USED:

USERNAME:

PASSWORD:

PIN:

NOTES:

NAME:

WEBSITE:

EMAIL USED:

USERNAME:

PASSWORD:

PIN:

NOTES:

NAME:

WEBSITE:

EMAIL USED:

USERNAME:

PASSWORD:

PIN:

NOTES:

NAME:

WEBSITE:

EMAIL USED:

USERNAME:

PASSWORD:

PIN:

NOTES:

NAME:

WEBSITE:

EMAIL USED:

USERNAME:

PASSWORD:

PIN:

NOTES:

NAME:

WEBSITE:

EMAIL USED:

USERNAME:

PASSWORD:

PIN:

NOTES:

NAME:

WEBSITE:

EMAIL USED:

USERNAME:

PASSWORD:

PIN:

NOTES:

....

....

NAME:

WEBSITE:

EMAIL USED:

USERNAME:

PASSWORD:

PIN:

NOTES:

....

....

NAME:

WEBSITE:

EMAIL USED:

USERNAME:

PASSWORD:

PIN:

NOTES:

....

....

NAME:

WEBSITE:

EMAIL USED:

USERNAME:

PASSWORD:

PIN:

NOTES:

....

....

....

NAME:

WEBSITE:

EMAIL USED:

USERNAME:

PASSWORD:

PIN:

NOTES:

....

....

....

NAME:

WEBSITE:

EMAIL USED:

USERNAME:

PASSWORD:

PIN:

NOTES:

....

....

....

NAME:

WEBSITE:

EMAIL USED:

USERNAME:

PASSWORD:

PIN:

NOTES:

NAME:

WEBSITE:

EMAIL USED:

USERNAME:

PASSWORD:

PIN:

NOTES:

NAME:

WEBSITE:

EMAIL USED:

USERNAME:

PASSWORD:

PIN:

NOTES:

NAME:

WEBSITE:

EMAIL USED:

USERNAME:

PASSWORD:

PIN:

NOTES:

NAME:

WEBSITE:

EMAIL USED:

USERNAME:

PASSWORD:

PIN:

NOTES:

NAME:

WEBSITE:

EMAIL USED:

USERNAME:

PASSWORD:

PIN:

NOTES:

NAME:

WEBSITE:

EMAIL USED:

USERNAME:

PASSWORD:

PIN:

NOTES:

NAME:

WEBSITE:

EMAIL USED:

USERNAME:

PASSWORD:

PIN:

NOTES:

NAME:

WEBSITE:

EMAIL USED:

USERNAME:

PASSWORD:

PIN:

NOTES:

NAME:

WEBSITE:

EMAIL USED:

USERNAME:

PASSWORD:

PIN:

NOTES:

NAME:

WEBSITE:

EMAIL USED:

USERNAME:

PASSWORD:

PIN:

NOTES:

NAME:

WEBSITE:

EMAIL USED:

USERNAME:

PASSWORD:

PIN:

NOTES:

NAME:

WEBSITE:

EMAIL USED:

USERNAME:

PASSWORD:

PIN:

NOTES:

NAME:

WEBSITE:

EMAIL USED:

USERNAME:

PASSWORD:

PIN:

NOTES:

NAME:

WEBSITE:

EMAIL USED:

USERNAME:

PASSWORD:

PIN:

NOTES:

NAME:

WEBSITE:

EMAIL USED:

USERNAME:

PASSWORD:

PIN:

NOTES:

....

....

NAME:

WEBSITE:

EMAIL USED:

USERNAME:

PASSWORD:

PIN:

NOTES:

....

....

NAME:

WEBSITE:

EMAIL USED:

USERNAME:

PASSWORD:

PIN:

NOTES:

....

....

NAME:

WEBSITE:

EMAIL USED:

USERNAME:

PASSWORD:

PIN:

NOTES:

NAME:

WEBSITE:

EMAIL USED:

USERNAME:

PASSWORD:

PIN:

NOTES:

NAME:

WEBSITE:

EMAIL USED:

USERNAME:

PASSWORD:

PIN:

NOTES:

NAME:

WEBSITE:

EMAIL USED:

USERNAME:

PASSWORD:

PIN:

NOTES:

....

....

....

NAME:

WEBSITE:

EMAIL USED:

USERNAME:

PASSWORD:

PIN:

NOTES:

....

....

....

NAME:

WEBSITE:

EMAIL USED:

USERNAME:

PASSWORD:

PIN:

NOTES:

....

....

....

NAME:

WEBSITE:

EMAIL USED:

USERNAME:

PASSWORD:

PIN:

NOTES:

NAME:

WEBSITE:

EMAIL USED:

USERNAME:

PASSWORD:

PIN:

NOTES:

NAME:

WEBSITE:

EMAIL USED:

USERNAME:

PASSWORD:

PIN:

NOTES:

NAME:

WEBSITE:

EMAIL USED:

USERNAME:

PASSWORD:

PIN:

NOTES:

NAME:

WEBSITE:

EMAIL USED:

USERNAME:

PASSWORD:

PIN:

NOTES:

NAME:

WEBSITE:

EMAIL USED:

USERNAME:

PASSWORD:

PIN:

NOTES:

NAME:

WEBSITE:

EMAIL USED:

USERNAME:

PASSWORD:

PIN:

NOTES:

NAME:

WEBSITE:

EMAIL USED:

USERNAME:

PASSWORD:

PIN:

NOTES:

NAME:

WEBSITE:

EMAIL USED:

USERNAME:

PASSWORD:

PIN:

NOTES:

NAME:

WEBSITE:

EMAIL USED:

USERNAME:

PASSWORD:

PIN:

NOTES:

NAME:

WEBSITE:

EMAIL USED:

USERNAME:

PASSWORD:

PIN:

NOTES:

NAME:

WEBSITE:

EMAIL USED:

USERNAME:

PASSWORD:

PIN:

NOTES:

NAME:

WEBSITE:

EMAIL USED:

USERNAME:

PASSWORD:

PIN:

NOTES:

....

....

....

NAME:

WEBSITE:

EMAIL USED:

USERNAME:

PASSWORD:

PIN:

NOTES:

....

....

....

NAME:

WEBSITE:

EMAIL USED:

USERNAME:

PASSWORD:

PIN:

NOTES:

....

....

....

NAME:

WEBSITE:

EMAIL USED:

USERNAME:

PASSWORD:

PIN:

NOTES:

NAME:

WEBSITE:

EMAIL USED:

USERNAME:

PASSWORD:

PIN:

NOTES:

NAME:

WEBSITE:

EMAIL USED:

USERNAME:

PASSWORD:

PIN:

NOTES:

NAME:

WEBSITE:

EMAIL USED:

USERNAME:

PASSWORD:

PIN:

NOTES:

NAME:

WEBSITE:

EMAIL USED:

USERNAME:

PASSWORD:

PIN:

NOTES:

NAME:

WEBSITE:

EMAIL USED:

USERNAME:

PASSWORD:

PIN:

NOTES:

NAME: _____

WEBSITE: _____

EMAIL USED: _____

USERNAME: _____

PASSWORD: _____

PIN: _____

NOTES: _____

_____

_____

NAME: _____

WEBSITE: _____

EMAIL USED: _____

USERNAME: _____

PASSWORD: _____

PIN: _____

NOTES: _____

_____

_____

NAME: _____

WEBSITE: _____

EMAIL USED: _____

USERNAME: _____

PASSWORD: _____

PIN: _____

NOTES: _____

_____

_____

K

NAME:

WEBSITE:

EMAIL USED:

USERNAME:

PASSWORD:

PIN:

NOTES:

NAME:

WEBSITE:

EMAIL USED:

USERNAME:

PASSWORD:

PIN:

NOTES:

NAME:

WEBSITE:

EMAIL USED:

USERNAME:

PASSWORD:

PIN:

NOTES:

NAME:

WEBSITE:

EMAIL USED:

USERNAME:

PASSWORD:

PIN:

NOTES:

NAME:

WEBSITE:

EMAIL USED:

USERNAME:

PASSWORD:

PIN:

NOTES:

NAME:

WEBSITE:

EMAIL USED:

USERNAME:

PASSWORD:

PIN:

NOTES:

NAME:

WEBSITE:

EMAIL USED:

USERNAME:

PASSWORD:

PIN:

NOTES:

NAME:

WEBSITE:

EMAIL USED:

USERNAME:

PASSWORD:

PIN:

NOTES:

NAME:

WEBSITE:

EMAIL USED:

USERNAME:

PASSWORD:

PIN:

NOTES:

NAME:

WEBSITE:

EMAIL USED:

USERNAME:

PASSWORD:

PIN:

NOTES:

NAME:

WEBSITE:

EMAIL USED:

USERNAME:

PASSWORD:

PIN:

NOTES:

NAME:

WEBSITE:

EMAIL USED:

USERNAME:

PASSWORD:

PIN:

NOTES:

NAME:

WEBSITE:

EMAIL USED:

USERNAME:

PASSWORD:

PIN:

NOTES:

NAME:

WEBSITE:

EMAIL USED:

USERNAME:

PASSWORD:

PIN:

NOTES:

NAME:

WEBSITE:

EMAIL USED:

USERNAME:

PASSWORD:

PIN:

NOTES:

NAME:

WEBSITE:

EMAIL USED:

USERNAME:

PASSWORD:

PIN:

NOTES:

NAME:

WEBSITE:

EMAIL USED:

USERNAME:

PASSWORD:

PIN:

NOTES:

NAME:

WEBSITE:

EMAIL USED:

USERNAME:

PASSWORD:

PIN:

NOTES:

NAME:

WEBSITE:

EMAIL USED:

USERNAME:

PASSWORD:

PIN:

NOTES:

NAME:

WEBSITE:

EMAIL USED:

USERNAME:

PASSWORD:

PIN:

NOTES:

NAME:

WEBSITE:

EMAIL USED:

USERNAME:

PASSWORD:

PIN:

NOTES:

NAME:

WEBSITE:

EMAIL USED:

USERNAME:

PASSWORD:

PIN:

NOTES:

NAME:

WEBSITE:

EMAIL USED:

USERNAME:

PASSWORD:

PIN:

NOTES:

NAME:

WEBSITE:

EMAIL USED:

USERNAME:

PASSWORD:

PIN:

NOTES:

NAME:

WEBSITE:

EMAIL USED:

USERNAME:

PASSWORD:

PIN:

NOTES:

....

....

....

NAME:

WEBSITE:

EMAIL USED:

USERNAME:

PASSWORD:

PIN:

NOTES:

....

....

....

NAME:

WEBSITE:

EMAIL USED:

USERNAME:

PASSWORD:

PIN:

NOTES:

....

....

....

NAME:

WEBSITE:

EMAIL USED:

USERNAME:

PASSWORD:

PIN:

NOTES:

NAME:

WEBSITE:

EMAIL USED:

USERNAME:

PASSWORD:

PIN:

NOTES:

NAME:

WEBSITE:

EMAIL USED:

USERNAME:

PASSWORD:

PIN:

NOTES:

NAME:

WEBSITE:

EMAIL USED:

USERNAME:

PASSWORD:

PIN:

NOTES:

NAME:

WEBSITE:

EMAIL USED:

USERNAME:

PASSWORD:

PIN:

NOTES:

NAME:

WEBSITE:

EMAIL USED:

USERNAME:

PASSWORD:

PIN:

NOTES:

NAME:

WEBSITE:

EMAIL USED:

USERNAME:

PASSWORD:

PIN:

NOTES:

NAME:

WEBSITE:

EMAIL USED:

USERNAME:

PASSWORD:

PIN:

NOTES:

NAME:

WEBSITE:

EMAIL USED:

USERNAME:

PASSWORD:

PIN:

NOTES:

NAME:

WEBSITE:

EMAIL USED:

USERNAME:

PASSWORD:

PIN:

NOTES:

NAME:

WEBSITE:

EMAIL USED:

USERNAME:

PASSWORD:

PIN:

NOTES:

NAME:

WEBSITE:

EMAIL USED:

USERNAME:

PASSWORD:

PIN:

NOTES:

NAME: _____

WEBSITE: _____

EMAIL USED: _____

USERNAME: _____

PASSWORD: _____

PIN: _____

NOTES: ....

....

....

NAME: _____

WEBSITE: _____

EMAIL USED: _____

USERNAME: _____

PASSWORD: _____

PIN: _____

NOTES: ....

....

....

NAME: _____

WEBSITE: _____

EMAIL USED: _____

USERNAME: _____

PASSWORD: _____

PIN: _____

NOTES: ....

....

....

NAME:

WEBSITE:

EMAIL USED:

USERNAME:

PASSWORD:

PIN:

NOTES:

NAME:

WEBSITE:

EMAIL USED:

USERNAME:

PASSWORD:

PIN:

NOTES:

NAME:

WEBSITE:

EMAIL USED:

USERNAME:

PASSWORD:

PIN:

NOTES:

NAME:

WEBSITE:

EMAIL USED:

USERNAME:

PASSWORD:

PIN:

NOTES:

NAME:

WEBSITE:

EMAIL USED:

USERNAME:

PASSWORD:

PIN:

NOTES:

NAME:

WEBSITE:

EMAIL USED:

USERNAME:

PASSWORD:

PIN:

NOTES:

NAME:

WEBSITE:

EMAIL USED:

USERNAME:

PASSWORD:

PIN:

NOTES:

NAME:

WEBSITE:

EMAIL USED:

USERNAME:

PASSWORD:

PIN:

NOTES:

NAME:

WEBSITE:

EMAIL USED:

USERNAME:

PASSWORD:

PIN:

NOTES:

NAME:

WEBSITE:

EMAIL USED:

USERNAME:

PASSWORD:

PIN:

NOTES:

NAME:

WEBSITE:

EMAIL USED:

USERNAME:

PASSWORD:

PIN:

NOTES:

NAME:

WEBSITE:

EMAIL USED:

USERNAME:

PASSWORD:

PIN:

NOTES:

NAME:

WEBSITE:

EMAIL USED:

USERNAME:

PASSWORD:

PIN:

NOTES:

NAME:

WEBSITE:

EMAIL USED:

USERNAME:

PASSWORD:

PIN:

NOTES:

NAME:

WEBSITE:

EMAIL USED:

USERNAME:

PASSWORD:

PIN:

NOTES:

NAME:

WEBSITE:

EMAIL USED:

USERNAME:

PASSWORD:

PIN:

NOTES:

NAME:

WEBSITE:

EMAIL USED:

USERNAME:

PASSWORD:

PIN:

NOTES:

NAME:

WEBSITE:

EMAIL USED:

USERNAME:

PASSWORD:

PIN:

NOTES:

NAME:

WEBSITE:

EMAIL USED:

USERNAME:

PASSWORD:

PIN:

NOTES:

NAME:

WEBSITE:

EMAIL USED:

USERNAME:

PASSWORD:

PIN:

NOTES:

NAME:

WEBSITE:

EMAIL USED:

USERNAME:

PASSWORD:

PIN:

NOTES:

NAME:

WEBSITE:

EMAIL USED:

USERNAME:

PASSWORD:

PIN:

NOTES:

NAME:

WEBSITE:

EMAIL USED:

USERNAME:

PASSWORD:

PIN:

NOTES:

NAME:

WEBSITE:

EMAIL USED:

USERNAME:

PASSWORD:

PIN:

NOTES:

NAME:

WEBSITE:

EMAIL USED:

USERNAME:

PASSWORD:

PIN:

NOTES:

NAME:

WEBSITE:

EMAIL USED:

USERNAME:

PASSWORD:

PIN:

NOTES:

NAME:

WEBSITE:

EMAIL USED:

USERNAME:

PASSWORD:

PIN:

NOTES:

NAME: _____

WEBSITE: _____

EMAIL USED: _____

USERNAME: _____

PASSWORD: _____

PIN: _____

NOTES: ....

....

....

NAME: _____

WEBSITE: _____

EMAIL USED: _____

USERNAME: _____

PASSWORD: _____

PIN: _____

NOTES: ....

....

....

NAME: _____

WEBSITE: _____

EMAIL USED: _____

USERNAME: _____

PASSWORD: _____

PIN: _____

NOTES: ....

....

....

NAME:

WEBSITE:

EMAIL USED:

USERNAME:

PASSWORD:

PIN:

NOTES:

NAME:

WEBSITE:

EMAIL USED:

USERNAME:

PASSWORD:

PIN:

NOTES:

NAME:

WEBSITE:

EMAIL USED:

USERNAME:

PASSWORD:

PIN:

NOTES:

NAME:

WEBSITE:

EMAIL USED:

USERNAME:

PASSWORD:

PIN:

NOTES:

NAME:

WEBSITE:

EMAIL USED:

USERNAME:

PASSWORD:

PIN:

NOTES:

NAME:

WEBSITE:

EMAIL USED:

USERNAME:

PASSWORD:

PIN:

NOTES:

NAME: _____

WEBSITE: _____

EMAIL USED: _____

USERNAME: _____

PASSWORD: _____

PIN: _____

NOTES: ....

....

....

NAME: _____

WEBSITE: _____

EMAIL USED: _____

USERNAME: _____

PASSWORD: _____

PIN: _____

NOTES: ....

....

....

NAME: _____

WEBSITE: _____

EMAIL USED: _____

USERNAME: _____

PASSWORD: _____

PIN: _____

NOTES: ....

....

....

R

NAME:

WEBSITE:

EMAIL USED:

USERNAME:

PASSWORD:

PIN:

NOTES:

NAME:

WEBSITE:

EMAIL USED:

USERNAME:

PASSWORD:

PIN:

NOTES:

NAME:

WEBSITE:

EMAIL USED:

USERNAME:

PASSWORD:

PIN:

NOTES:

NAME:

WEBSITE:

EMAIL USED:

USERNAME:

PASSWORD:

PIN:

NOTES:

NAME:

WEBSITE:

EMAIL USED:

USERNAME:

PASSWORD:

PIN:

NOTES:

NAME:

WEBSITE:

EMAIL USED:

USERNAME:

PASSWORD:

PIN:

NOTES:

NAME:

WEBSITE:

EMAIL USED:

USERNAME:

PASSWORD:

PIN:

NOTES:

NAME:

WEBSITE:

EMAIL USED:

USERNAME:

PASSWORD:

PIN:

NOTES:

NAME:

WEBSITE:

EMAIL USED:

USERNAME:

PASSWORD:

PIN:

NOTES:

NAME:

WEBSITE:

EMAIL USED:

USERNAME:

PASSWORD:

PIN:

NOTES:

NAME:

WEBSITE:

EMAIL USED:

USERNAME:

PASSWORD:

PIN:

NOTES:

NAME:

WEBSITE:

EMAIL USED:

USERNAME:

PASSWORD:

PIN:

NOTES:

NAME:

WEBSITE:

EMAIL USED:

USERNAME:

PASSWORD:

PIN:

NOTES:

NAME:

WEBSITE:

EMAIL USED:

USERNAME:

PASSWORD:

PIN:

NOTES:

NAME:

WEBSITE:

EMAIL USED:

USERNAME:

PASSWORD:

PIN:

NOTES:

NAME:

WEBSITE:

EMAIL USED:

USERNAME:

PASSWORD:

PIN:

NOTES:

....

....

NAME:

WEBSITE:

EMAIL USED:

USERNAME:

PASSWORD:

PIN:

NOTES:

....

....

NAME:

WEBSITE:

EMAIL USED:

USERNAME:

PASSWORD:

PIN:

NOTES:

....

....

NAME:

WEBSITE:

EMAIL USED:

USERNAME:

PASSWORD:

PIN:

NOTES:

....

....

....

NAME:

WEBSITE:

EMAIL USED:

USERNAME:

PASSWORD:

PIN:

NOTES:

....

....

....

NAME:

WEBSITE:

EMAIL USED:

USERNAME:

PASSWORD:

PIN:

NOTES:

....

....

....

NAME:

WEBSITE:

EMAIL USED:

USERNAME:

PASSWORD:

PIN:

NOTES:

NAME:

WEBSITE:

EMAIL USED:

USERNAME:

PASSWORD:

PIN:

NOTES:

NAME:

WEBSITE:

EMAIL USED:

USERNAME:

PASSWORD:

PIN:

NOTES:

NAME:

WEBSITE:

EMAIL USED:

USERNAME:

PASSWORD:

PIN:

NOTES:

NAME:

WEBSITE:

EMAIL USED:

USERNAME:

PASSWORD:

PIN:

NOTES:

NAME:

WEBSITE:

EMAIL USED:

USERNAME:

PASSWORD:

PIN:

NOTES:

NAME:

WEBSITE:

EMAIL USED:

USERNAME:

PASSWORD:

PIN:

NOTES:

NAME:

WEBSITE:

EMAIL USED:

USERNAME:

PASSWORD:

PIN:

NOTES:

NAME:

WEBSITE:

EMAIL USED:

USERNAME:

PASSWORD:

PIN:

NOTES:

NAME:

WEBSITE:

EMAIL USED:

USERNAME:

PASSWORD:

PIN:

NOTES:

NAME:

WEBSITE:

EMAIL USED:

USERNAME:

PASSWORD:

PIN:

NOTES:

NAME:

WEBSITE:

EMAIL USED:

USERNAME:

PASSWORD:

PIN:

NOTES:

NAME:

WEBSITE:

EMAIL USED:

USERNAME:

PASSWORD:

PIN:

NOTES:

NAME:

WEBSITE:

EMAIL USED:

USERNAME:

PASSWORD:

PIN:

NOTES:

NAME:

WEBSITE:

EMAIL USED:

USERNAME:

PASSWORD:

PIN:

NOTES:

NAME: _____

WEBSITE: _____

EMAIL USED: _____

USERNAME: _____

PASSWORD: _____

PIN: _____

NOTES: ....

....

....

NAME: _____

WEBSITE: _____

EMAIL USED: _____

USERNAME: _____

PASSWORD: _____

PIN: _____

NOTES: ....

....

....

NAME: _____

WEBSITE: _____

EMAIL USED: _____

USERNAME: _____

PASSWORD: _____

PIN: _____

NOTES: ....

....

....

NAME:

WEBSITE:

EMAIL USED:

USERNAME:

PASSWORD:

PIN:

NOTES:

NAME:

WEBSITE:

EMAIL USED:

USERNAME:

PASSWORD:

PIN:

NOTES:

NAME:

WEBSITE:

EMAIL USED:

USERNAME:

PASSWORD:

PIN:

NOTES:

V

NAME: _____

WEBSITE: _____

EMAIL USED: _____

USERNAME: _____

PASSWORD: _____

PIN: _____

NOTES: _____

_____

_____

NAME: _____

WEBSITE: _____

EMAIL USED: _____

USERNAME: _____

PASSWORD: _____

PIN: _____

NOTES: _____

_____

_____

NAME: _____

WEBSITE: _____

EMAIL USED: _____

USERNAME: _____

PASSWORD: _____

PIN: _____

NOTES: _____

_____

_____

NAME:

WEBSITE:

EMAIL USED:

USERNAME:

PASSWORD:

PIN:

NOTES:

NAME:

WEBSITE:

EMAIL USED:

USERNAME:

PASSWORD:

PIN:

NOTES:

NAME:

WEBSITE:

EMAIL USED:

USERNAME:

PASSWORD:

PIN:

NOTES:

NAME:

WEBSITE:

EMAIL USED:

USERNAME:

PASSWORD:

PIN:

NOTES:

NAME:

WEBSITE:

EMAIL USED:

USERNAME:

PASSWORD:

PIN:

NOTES:

NAME:

WEBSITE:

EMAIL USED:

USERNAME:

PASSWORD:

PIN:

NOTES:

NAME:

WEBSITE:

EMAIL USED:

USERNAME:

PASSWORD:

PIN:

NOTES:

NAME:

WEBSITE:

EMAIL USED:

USERNAME:

PASSWORD:

PIN:

NOTES:

NAME:

WEBSITE:

EMAIL USED:

USERNAME:

PASSWORD:

PIN:

NOTES:

NAME:

WEBSITE:

EMAIL USED:

USERNAME:

PASSWORD:

PIN:

NOTES:

NAME:

WEBSITE:

EMAIL USED:

USERNAME:

PASSWORD:

PIN:

NOTES:

NAME:

WEBSITE:

EMAIL USED:

USERNAME:

PASSWORD:

PIN:

NOTES:

NAME:

WEBSITE:

EMAIL USED:

USERNAME:

PASSWORD:

PIN:

NOTES:

NAME:

WEBSITE:

EMAIL USED:

USERNAME:

PASSWORD:

PIN:

NOTES:

NAME:

WEBSITE:

EMAIL USED:

USERNAME:

PASSWORD:

PIN:

NOTES:

NAME:

WEBSITE:

EMAIL USED:

USERNAME:

PASSWORD:

PIN:

NOTES:

NAME:

WEBSITE:

EMAIL USED:

USERNAME:

PASSWORD:

PIN:

NOTES:

NAME:

WEBSITE:

EMAIL USED:

USERNAME:

PASSWORD:

PIN:

NOTES:

NAME:

WEBSITE:

EMAIL USED:

USERNAME:

PASSWORD:

PIN:

NOTES:

NAME:

WEBSITE:

EMAIL USED:

USERNAME:

PASSWORD:

PIN:

NOTES:

NAME:

WEBSITE:

EMAIL USED:

USERNAME:

PASSWORD:

PIN:

NOTES:

NAME:

WEBSITE:

EMAIL USED:

USERNAME:

PASSWORD:

PIN:

NOTES:

NAME:

WEBSITE:

EMAIL USED:

USERNAME:

PASSWORD:

PIN:

NOTES:

NAME:

WEBSITE:

EMAIL USED:

USERNAME:

PASSWORD:

PIN:

NOTES:

NAME:

WEBSITE:

EMAIL USED:

USERNAME:

PASSWORD:

PIN:

NOTES:

NAME:

WEBSITE:

EMAIL USED:

USERNAME:

PASSWORD:

PIN:

NOTES:

NAME:

WEBSITE:

EMAIL USED:

USERNAME:

PASSWORD:

PIN:

NOTES:

NAME:

WEBSITE:

EMAIL USED:

USERNAME:

PASSWORD:

PIN:

NOTES:

NAME:

WEBSITE:

EMAIL USED:

USERNAME:

PASSWORD:

PIN:

NOTES:

NAME:

WEBSITE:

EMAIL USED:

USERNAME:

PASSWORD:

PIN:

NOTES:

NAME:

WEBSITE:

EMAIL USED:

USERNAME:

PASSWORD:

PIN:

NOTES:

NAME:

WEBSITE:

EMAIL USED:

USERNAME:

PASSWORD:

PIN:

NOTES:

NAME:

WEBSITE:

EMAIL USED:

USERNAME:

PASSWORD:

PIN:

NOTES:

NAME:

WEBSITE:

EMAIL USED:

USERNAME:

PASSWORD:

PIN:

NOTES:

NAME:

WEBSITE:

EMAIL USED:

USERNAME:

PASSWORD:

PIN:

NOTES:

NAME:

WEBSITE:

EMAIL USED:

USERNAME:

PASSWORD:

PIN:

NOTES:

NAME:

WEBSITE:

EMAIL USED:

USERNAME:

PASSWORD:

PIN:

NOTES:

NAME:

WEBSITE:

EMAIL USED:

USERNAME:

PASSWORD:

PIN:

NOTES:

NAME:

WEBSITE:

EMAIL USED:

USERNAME:

PASSWORD:

PIN:

NOTES:

NAME:

WEBSITE:

EMAIL USED:

USERNAME:

PASSWORD:

PIN:

NOTES:

....

....

NAME:

WEBSITE:

EMAIL USED:

USERNAME:

PASSWORD:

PIN:

NOTES:

....

....

NAME:

WEBSITE:

EMAIL USED:

USERNAME:

PASSWORD:

PIN:

NOTES:

....

....

NAME:

WEBSITE:

EMAIL USED:

USERNAME:

PASSWORD:

PIN:

NOTES:

NAME:

WEBSITE:

EMAIL USED:

USERNAME:

PASSWORD:

PIN:

NOTES:

NAME:

WEBSITE:

EMAIL USED:

USERNAME:

PASSWORD:

PIN:

NOTES:

NAME:

WEBSITE:

EMAIL USED:

USERNAME:

PASSWORD:

PIN:

NOTES:

....

....

NAME:

WEBSITE:

EMAIL USED:

USERNAME:

PASSWORD:

PIN:

NOTES:

....

....

NAME:

WEBSITE:

EMAIL USED:

USERNAME:

PASSWORD:

PIN:

NOTES:

....

....

NAME:

WEBSITE:

EMAIL USED:

USERNAME:

PASSWORD:

PIN:

NOTES:

NAME:

WEBSITE:

EMAIL USED:

USERNAME:

PASSWORD:

PIN:

NOTES:

NAME:

WEBSITE:

EMAIL USED:

USERNAME:

PASSWORD:

PIN:

NOTES:

NAME:

WEBSITE:

EMAIL USED:

USERNAME:

PASSWORD:

PIN:

NOTES:

....

....

....

NAME:

WEBSITE:

EMAIL USED:

USERNAME:

PASSWORD:

PIN:

NOTES:

....

....

....

NAME:

WEBSITE:

EMAIL USED:

USERNAME:

PASSWORD:

PIN:

NOTES:

....

....

....

EXTRA NOTES

EXTRA NOTES

....
....
....
....
....
....
....
....
....
....
....
....
....
....
....
....
....
....
....
....
....
....
....
....

Made in United States
North Haven, CT
09 October 2022

25187560R00065